A Taste of Guam

Collections of Guam dishes

and

Other favorite recipes.

Written by Paula A. Lujan Quinene
Photographed by Edward J. Quinene

MW00453604

Copyright © 2006 by Paula A. Lujan Quinene

All rights reserved. No part of this book shall be reproduced or transmitted in any form or by any means, electronic, mechanical, magnetic, photographic including photocopying, recording or by any information storage and retrieval system, without prior written permission of the publisher. No patent liability is assumed with respect to the use of the information contained herein. Although every precaution has been taken in the preparation of this book, the publisher and author assume no responsibility for errors or omissions. Neither is any liability assumed for damages resulting from the use of the information contained herein.

ISBN 978-0-7414-3368-8

Published by:

1094 New DeHaven Street, Suite 100
West Conshohocken, PA 19428-2713
Info@buybooksontheweb.com
www.buybooksontheweb.com
Toll-free (877) BUY BOOK
Local Phone (610) 941-9999
Fax (610) 941-9959

Printed in the United States of America
Published October 2012

In honor of my grandparents

Nieves & Quirino Cabe

Terrisita & Jesus Cruz

For without them I would not have my cherished memories.

In memory of my Grandpa Cruz and Grandpa Cabe, whom I will someday meet again, I miss you both!!

And my parents

Maureen & Paul Lujan

Whose guidance and support have given me the confidence to accomplish my goals.

Dedication

This book is dedicated to my husband Sonny, who I dearly love and has stood by me the last ten years; to my precious children, Carson, my son, who amazes me everyday with his words, his thoughts and his actions; Evalie, my daughter, who exudes brilliance, confidence and humor; to my siblings Jun, Mark, Pearl, Steven and Timmy, whom I look forward to raising our children together, whom I am exceedingly proud of, whom I miss so very much; to my brother-in-law Lee who I am grateful keeps us all in touch; for my sister-in-laws Colleen, Jasmine and Yolynn, whom I just love; to my aunties, uncles, and cousins, who gave me the best homecoming and farewell a girl could ask for; to my family in the last ten years, mom and dad, Doris & Ed Quinene, who are wonderful, welcoming and considerate; siblings Trish & Rocky, who are great godparents; Jackie, whom I am so proud of her accomplishments; Robbi who is a jack of all trades; to our family in South Carolina, nina and nino, Daling & Kin Quinene, who always think of us; cousins Vanessa & James, so giving of themselves and their home; to Nina's sisters, spouses and children, Auntie Vivian and Auntie Doris, who opened their arms to us; to Nancy and Scott White, who have been our saving grace; to my nieces and nephews Trina, Triston, Perlene, Izaiah, Janessa, Jalynn, Mariana, Christopher, Michael and Victoria, who I am excited to watch grow up and reach for their dreams; to my eldest goddaughter Kalani, who I am absolutely proud of; to my closest friends, the best a girl could ever have, Jennifer Cruz, Melonie Quintanilla, Cheryl Meregillano, Lorilyn Mendoza, and Nancy White; and finally, to my new friends Shelly Rickert and Melanie Tucker, whom I look forward to making memories with.

Contents

Guam Desserts

Mix of America

Treasure Chest of Sweets

Guam, Where America's Day Begins

Acknowledgment

My thanks to everyone who has helped me with this book! Dankolo na si Yu'us Ma'ase to my husband who took the pictures! Dankolo na si Yu'us Ma'ase to the friends and family who shared their recipes, tips and techniques.

Foreword

My sister Pearl and I were strolling through the isles of Barnes & Noble. Suddenly, a brilliant idea revealed itself: to write a Guam cookbook!! We sifted through the shelves of the bookstore and did not find anything on Guam. I searched the internet and came up with zilch. Thereafter, the production ensued for *A Taste of Guam.*

I wanted to write a recipe book that had Chamorro recipes most people were familiar with and could replicate. Typically, when I make Chamorro food I do not measure. In preparing this recipe book, I actually cooked up a storm one weekend recording all the tablespoons of lemon powder, salt, soy sauce etc. As a result, the recipes used in this cookbook have accurate measurements. Remember, however, that you still have to adjust the seasonings to your taste and the environment you are cooking in.

I also thought it would be great to include other delicious recipes I have accumulated over the years. Hence, the book is divided into the following collections: Chamorro BBQ, Other Island Favorites, Guam Desserts, Mix of America and Treasure Chest of Sweets.

Hafa Adai!

Thank you for picking up a copy of *A Taste of Guam*! I hope you will find this a great resource of foods typically found at Chamorro bbqs and on the kitchen tables of Chamorro families.

For the longest time, I aspired to be a pastry chef. Dessert was king and came before breakfast, lunch or dinner. At parties, it was latiya or roskette before red rice and ribs. So, when I write that a particular dessert was the best I have ever had, I really mean it!

I have added a few pages of fun and useful information related to the recipes and to Guam in general. If you have ever been to Guam, I hope you had an awesome stay!! If you will be going to Guam, enjoy my island and remember to visit the southern end, as it is in the South where Guam's beauty has been preserved!

Check-out cooking demonstrations for *A Taste of Guam* at www.paulaq.com. You may also e-mail Paula at pquinene@paulaq.com with any questions.

CHAMORRO

BBQ

A collection of foods at a Chamorro bbq

RED RICE

"The red rice my mom makes is so delicious: the flavor of the achote (annatto) seed, nuances of garlic....yummmm!! Even to this day, hers is the best pot of red rice I have ever had!"

INGREDIENTS / DIRECTIONS

Set 1
5 c. Calrose style rice
(short grain, sticky rice)

Set 2
5 ½ c. water
4 T. vegetable oil
1 T. pork fat
   (bacon drippings)
      or 2 T. sliced bacon (opt.)
¼ c. yellow onion, chopped
1½ t. garlic powder
¾ t. salt & ½ t. black pepper
5 t. seasoning salt

Set 3
7 T. achote seeds

Tools: *strainer,*   *medium pot*

1. In a medium pot, measure / rinse 5 cups rice. [A] Add 5 ¼ cups water (more water may be necessary while the rice cooks). Use the same measuring cup for the water and the rice.

2. Add oil, pork fat and onions. Season to taste with seasoning salt, pepper, garlic powder and salt so that it is quite flavorful.

3. Set pot on medium high heat.

4. Place strainer over pot such that it is about 2 inches submerged into the liquid. Put achote seeds into the strainer. As liquid heats, the color / flavor will be released. Stir seeds within the strainer constantly. Let boil for 10 minutes, long enough to get a dark orange, almost red color. Stir the pot of rice occasionally to prevent the bottom from sticking and burning.

5. After coloring is completed, remove strainer with the seeds. If more seasoning is necessary, adjust accordingly (primarily seasoning salt and garlic powder).

6. At this time, if it looks like much of the water has been absorbed, add ¼ cup more water.

7. Stir rice. Cover the rice and allow to steam.

8. After 10 minutes, check rice. If kernels are cooking and rice looks to have enough water, scoop rice. [B] Cover and let steam for another 15 minutes or till done. HOWEVER, **if kernels are still quite opaque** and rice looks dry, add ½ cup more water. Let steam for 10 minutes. Check rice again.

HELPFUL HINTS

A. Calrose style rice gives the red rice its' best taste and texture!! Short / medium grain rice is also better for leftovers the next day. If long grain rice is used, more water is necessary, check instructions on the bag. Also, long grain is not as great the next day. However, for best results with long grain leftovers, sprinkle a little bit of water over rice, heat on high for a minute, or as needed. The end result will be soft rice, albeit not clumpy / sticky like short grain rice.

B. When cooking the rice, do not stir once most of the liquid has been absorbed. Scoop the rice to prevent the rice from becoming a glob of mush!! The end product should have soft, distinct kernels with a sheen from the oil.

BBQ MEAT

"We love our bbq!! There is nothing like marinating ribs with mostly soy sauce and vinegar. I love my bbq strong, and that means it marinades for 24 hours!"

INGREDIENTS / DIRECTIONS

Set 1
1 c. soy sauce
1 c. vinegar
¼ c. to ½ c. brown sugar
2 t. garlic powder
½ onion, sliced
½ t. salt
½ t. pepper
½ c. water (optional)

Set 2
ribs, chicken, steak, pork belly, etc.

Tools: *large plastic container, bbq necessities*

1. In plastic container, combine all ingredients. Adjust sugar to taste.
2. Place meat into marinade and let it sit over night.

The meat of choice does need to marinate at least 12 hours to get the best, full flavor!!

I like my bbq on the sweeter side, therefore I use ¾ c. brown sugar.

PANCIT

"Wonderful on its own or with bbq!"

INGREDIENTS / DIRECTIONS

Set 1
16 oz. canton noodles
   (yellow egg noodles)

Set 2
4 T. vegetable oil
½ c. chopped onion

Set 3
2 lbs. tender meat
   (pork, chicken,
   beef or shrimp
   or combo)
2 T. white wine
¼ t. black pepper
4 T. Mr. Yoshida's
   sauce
1 T. soy sauce

Set 4
¼ head of cabbage, shredded
¼ c. julienned carrots
¼ c. sliced celery
¼ c. green bell pepper, sliced 1 inch long
1 – 14 oz. can chicken stock

Tools: *large pot, tong*

1. In large pot, sauté onions in oil. In same pot, sauté meat and brown.
2. Add Mr. Yoshida's sauce, soy sauce, white wine, and black pepper.
3. Stir and cook for 8-10 minutes or till meat is done.
4. Add cabbage, carrots, celery and bell pepper. Stir till vegetables are soft. Add a ½ cup of chicken stock.

5. Press on the bag gently to break the noodles. Set the noodles on top of the meat / veggies. Cover the pot for 2-3 minutes. DO NOT OPEN. This will soften the noodles!

6. After 3 minutes open the pot and stir to combine. If the mixture is dry, add the remaining stock and more oil; stir. Reduce heat to medium-low and cover for 2 more minutes.

POTATO SALAD

"This rendition, which is typical at most Chamorro parties, is not tangy like the stateside version. I love this recipe, though some folks choose to add finely diced carrots and celery."

INGREDIENTS / DIRECTIONS

Set 1
5 lbs. russet potatoes
1 doz. eggs

Set 2
¼ c. dill relish, drained
¼ c. diced olives, drained
2 T. chopped pimentos
¼ t. garlic powder
2 c. mayonnaise
Dash of salt & pepper

Set 3
1 whole, cooked
   peeled, egg
a few sliced olives
a few slivers
   of pimentos

Tools: *large pot, small pot, large bowl*

1. Boil potatoes and eggs separately; peel and discard skins. Into a large bowl, chop potatoes into bite size pieces. Cut eggs into a smaller size compared to the potatoes and place into the same bowl.

2. Press relish, olives and pimentos through a sieve, one at a time to drain. Add to #1. Cool in the fridge.

3. Add enough mayonnaise to taste. Sprinkle in some garlic powder; add a few dashes of salt and pepper. Adjust accordingly.

4. Smooth the top of the salad and apply a thin layer of mayonnaise. Decorate with sliced/halved eggs, olives and pimentos.

CRAB AND BROCCOLI SALAD

"This is a refreshing change from potato salad, particularly when it is quite cold."

INGREDIENTS / DIRECTIONS

Set 1
1 – 12 oz. pkg. imitation crab sticks
4 c. chopped broccoli florets

Set 2
½ - 1 c. mayo
¼ t. black pepper
¼ t. garlic powder
1/8 t. salt

Tools: med. pot,   colander,   large bowl

1. Soften broccoli by placing florets in a pot of very hot water for 2-3 minutes. Drain and cool uncovered.
2. Cut crabsticks in half lengthwise and into 1.5 inch pieces. Shred with fingers into a large bowl.
3. Combine crab and broccoli. Add mayonnaise, little by little. Salad should be moist, not swimming in mayo.
4. Add salt, pepper, and garlic powder. Mix to combine.

CHICKEN KELAGUEN

(ke-la-gwen)

"In general, kelaguen is more tangy than salty and can be moist or dry. It is quite versatile to eat with titiyas, tortillas, siopao dough, white rice and of course, bbq food."

INGREDIENTS / DIRECTIONS

Set 1	Set 2	Set 3
16 c. cooked, chopped chicken	6 T. lemon powder	1 c. shredded, fresh
2 c. chopped, yellow onion	2 t. salt	coconut
3/4 c. chopped, green onion	hot pepper	
	½ c. water	

Tools: *machete or cleaver, kamyo, large bowl*

1. Combine the cooked chicken and onions in a large bowl. **A**
2. Add lemon powder, salt, hot pepper and water. Adjust to taste, should be more lemony than salty.
3. If using shredded coconut, add it to the mix and adjust to taste. **B**
4. Add more water if you like your kelaguen very moist.

HELPFUL HINTS

A. The chicken may be cooked using the following methods: boil, bake, bbq.

B. Crack the coconut in half by using a heavy duty knife to rap at the center of the nut. Rotate the nut in the palm of the hand after each rap. Use a kamyo (kum-dzu) to shred the coconut. Kelaguen is delicious with coconut, though it also tastes great without it. Keep in mind that in the fridge, kelaguen without coconut lasts longer than kelaguen with coconut.

IMITATION CRAB KELAGUEN

"Crab kelaguen is easier to make than chicken kelaguen, hence I make this more often."

INGREDIENTS / DIRECTIONS

Set 1
2 lbs. imitation crab sticks

Set 2
3 t. lemon powder
1 t. salt
¾ c. chopped, yellow onions
¼ c. chopped, green onions
¼ t. hot pepper
1 ½ c. water

Tools: *large bowl*

1. Slice crab sticks in half crosswise and then lengthwise. Shred crab with fingers and place in large plastic bowl.
2. Add to the crab lemon powder, pepper, salt, and the onions.
3. Pour in the water and stir.
4. Adjust lemon powder, salt and hot pepper to taste.

HELPFUL HINTS

The crab sticks are preferable to the crab chunks. These chunks do not have the same texture as the crab sticks.

LUMPIA

(lewm-pia)

"There are so many variations for lumpia filling. Here is my basic recipe which tastes great on its own and even better dipped in fina'denne'.

INGREDIENTS / DIRECTIONS

<u>Set 1</u>
1 T. oil
6 cloves garlic, minced
1 c. chopped, yellow onions
2 lbs. ground turkey
1 lb. ground pork

<u>Set 2</u>
¾ head of cabbage, shredded
2 ½ c. julienned carrots

<u>Set 3</u>
1 T. Yoshida's sauce
2 T. oyster sauce
7 T. soy sauce
1 t. pepper
1 t. seasoning salt

<u>Set 4</u>
6 T. flour + 6 T. water, mixed
2 boxes lumpia wrapper

Tools: *colander,   large pot,   pastry brush,   small cup*

1. In a large pot, sautee the garlic and onions. Add ground meat and brown. Stir continuously to get a fine crumble for the meat. Incorporate vegetables and cook to soften. Add dry and liquid seasonings. Adjust to taste.

2. Pour filling into the colander to cool and drain.

3. Once filling is cooled, separate lumpia wrappers.[A] Spoon 4 tablespoons of the filling onto the nearest edge of the wrapper. Fold burrito style. Moisten the open edge of the wrapper with the flour paste.

4. Line up lumpia on a cookie sheet and allow to dry.

5. When dried, layer lumpia in a freezer bag separated with wax paper.

6. Freeze lumpia before frying.

7. On medium to medium-high, heat a pot of oil for deep frying.

8. Fry frozen lumpia till browned on the outside and cooked on the inside.

HELPFUL HINTS

A. The wrappers dry quickly once the package is opened. Keep them moist by dividing each stack in half. Put one half in the original package or a zip-lock. Work quickly to fill and roll each wrapper. You may separate and roll 3-5 at a time. Dry wrappers tend to crack/tear more easily.

GOLLAI APPAN AGA

(gogh-lie aw-pan a-ga)

"This is a great dish on its own or with a bbq plate!"

INGREDIENTS / DIRECTIONS

Set 1
3 ripe plantains
1 – 13.5 oz. can coconut milk
2 T. sugar
cinnamon

Tools: *med. pot*

1. Slice plantains, with skin on, crosswise then lengthwise. This will yield 12 long slices.
2. Peel the skins off.
3. Place in cold pot. Shake the can of milk and pour into pot, covering plantains half way. Add sugar and cinnamon to taste. Stir then cover pot.
4. Simmer plantains over medium heat till fruit is softened, decreasing the heat so coconut milk does not boil.
5. Rearrange slices at least twice to prevent sticking.

TITIYAS

(ti-tee-dzas)

"I had the opportunity to make flour titiyas with Auntie Bea Fabellano. She had the best idea for titiyas: roll the dough out and cut with the smallest pot cover, 4-5 in. diameter. Cook accordingly. When you are ready to eat it (even out of the freezer), pop it in the toaster!!!! Smear with butter and jelly, yummmmm!"

INGREDIENTS / DIRECTIONS

Set 1	Set 2	Set 3
3 c. flour	3 T. butter, melted	2 c. whole, cold
¾ c. sugar	1 T. whole milk	milk
3 ¼ t. baking powder		

Tools: *large bowl, non-stick sauté pan, rolling pin, flour for dusting*

1. Combine all dry ingredients in large bowl.
2. Mix melted butter and 1 tablespoon milk. Sprinkle over dry ingredients and mix with fingers.
3. Add enough cold milk, a little at a time, to make a slightly sticky dough; you will not use all of the milk. Knead a few minutes. [A]
4. Roll out dough on a lightly floured surface, with a floured rolling pin. Dough thickness should be about ¼ in. thick. Cut with pot cover (optional) and punch the dough with fork tines.
5. Cook titiyas on a dry, non-stick pan, medium heat.
6. Once nicely browned, flip to cook on the other side. Check for doneness.
7. Cool on a wire rack. [B] Freeze or slice and serve.

HELPFUL HINTS

A. Knead dough only to completely combine all the ingredients (less than 5 minutes.)   It is unnecessary to knead the dough into oblivion!!

B. Once titiyas is cooled, wrap with plastic wrap and heavy-duty foil. When ready to eat, pop into the toaster.

FINA'DENNE'

(fi-na-de-knee)

"Looking for the ultimate sauce? This is it! Fina'denne' may be used to marinate raw meat, dip lumpia into, spoon over rice, spoon over cooked meat----yum! The green onions and tomatoes are optional, but they are a great addition."

INGREDIENTS / DIRECTIONS

<u>Set 1</u>
¼ c. diced onions
2 T. green onions
halved grape tomatoes
pinch of salt
¼ t. hot pepper

<u>Set 1 cont.</u>
½ c. soysauce
½ c. vinegar (white vinegar or
apple cider or lemon juice or
a combination)

Tools: *small glass dish*

1. Combine all ingredients and stir, adding more soy sauce / hot pepper if desired.

The best time to eat this is after the onions have soaked up the sauce.

DAIGO

(dy-gu)

"We love to pickle a lot of things on Guam: radish (daigo), rakyio (pearl onions), papaya, mango. Daigo is likely the most popular pickled item. My dad used to always have this with his meals. It is quite easy to make."

INGREDIENTS / INSTRUCTIONS

Set 1
1 pkg. yellow dyed radish (available in Asian stores)
2 T. sugar
1 c. vinegar
1 ¾ c. water + daigo juice
¾ t. salt
½ t. hot pepper (dried pepper flakes will work)

Tools: *med. glass or plastic bowl*

1. Open the bag of radish, POUR the yellow liquid into the bowl and SAVE.
2. Slice the radish into whole, thin circles, or thin semi-circles.
3. Add slices to #1 liquid. Add vinegar, water, sugar and pepper.
4. Adjust to taste.

OTHER ISLAND FAVORITES

Dishes typical in a Chamorro home

BISTEK

(bis-take)

"This dish can be a bit strong in taste, so eat a lot of white rice and enjoy!!"

INGREDIENTS / DIRECTIONS

<u>Set 1</u>
¾ c. soy sauce
½ c. vinegar
¼ c. water
½ onion, sliced
¼ t. salt
¼ t. pepper
½ t. garlic powder

<u>Set 2</u>
2 ½ lbs. top sirloin

<u>Set 3</u>
½ onion, sliced
4 cloves garlic,
    minced

Tools: *medium bowl, large sauté pan*

1. Make the marinade in a medium bowl by combining all of set 1.
2. Rinse the sirloin then cut into 1 ½ inch long strips, 1 centimeter thick. Marinade in #1 for 45 minutes.
3. Sautee garlic and remaining onions. Add meat and sauté. Add 1 cup of marinade to the pot and simmer till liquid is slightly reduced.

CORN SOUP

"This is wonderful on a cold day!! But, on Guam, it's great all the time."

INGREDIENTS / DIRECTIONS

Set 1
1 c. chopped onions
7 boneless, skinless chicken
   thighs, uncooked, chopped
4 T. butter
4 T. flour

Set 2
1 – 10 ¾ oz. can condensed, cream of mushroom soup + 1
   can water
2 – 13.5 oz. cans thick coconut milk, warm
2 – 15 oz. cans sweet corn, drained
1 – 14.5 oz. can chicken broth, hot
2 t. salt
½ t. pepper

Tools: *large pot,   whisk*

1. Melt butter in large pot on medium heat. Sautee onions till translucent. Add chicken and sauté till cooked.
2. Sprinkle 4 tablespoons of flour over the chicken/onions.
3. Pour 1 can of chicken broth into the pot and whisk quickly.
4. Add the cream of mushroom. Fill that can with water and add to the pot.
5. Using a whisk, stir till well combined.
6. Add salt and pepper.
7. Empty 2 cans of corn and coconut milk into the pot.
8. Continue to keep very hot without boiling for 10 more minutes.
9. Served best by itself.

CORN BEEF WITH CABBAGE

"Here is another favorite for many Chamorros. It is especially great with fina' denne' over hot white rice."

INGREDIENTS / DIRECTIONS

Set 1	Set 2	Set 3
½ onion, chopped	¼ head of cabbage, chopped	½ T. soy sauce
2 cans corn beef		¼ t. black pepper

Tools*: large sauté pan*

1. Sautee onions in large pot. Add corn beef and brown.
2. Add cabbage, cook till softened. Add soy sauce and black pepper to taste.

DEVILED EGG SANDWICHES

*"I remember my cousins and I walking down
grandma Cabe's steps, each with a sandwich in hand, a dab of ketchup, lots of
filling.....ymmmm!!"*

INGREDIENTS / DIRECTIONS

<u>Set 1</u>   <u>Set 2</u>
1 doz. eggs   white sandwich bread
mayo   ketchup
salt & pepper

Tools: *medium pot,   medium bowl*

1. Boil the eggs. Drain water. Rinse eggs under cold running water for a minute. Peel and chop the eggs into medium bowl.
2. Add enough mayo to make a nice, chunky filling, not too wet with mayonnaise. Add salt & pepper to taste.
3. Lather filling on bread and dab with ketchup if desired.

ESTUFAO

(es-to-fau)

"This is a favorite dinner item in most households. I've been making this since my first year into college. However, two years ago, my mom taught me the best way to make it."

INGREDIENTS / DIRECTIONS

Set 1
1 c. soy sauce
1 c. vinegar
¼ c. water
½ onion, chopped
1 t. garlic powder
¼ t. salt
¼ t. pepper

Set 2
4 lbs. wings / drummets
    (If frozen soak overnight
covered in water and 4T. salt)

Set 3
3 cloves garlic,
  minced
½ onion, chopped

Tools: large pot

1. Combine the soy sauce, vinegar, water, garlic powder, half of the onions, salt and pepper, stir. Add the chicken and let marinate for 4-6 hours.
2. Sautee the garlic and remaining onions. Remove the chicken and onions from the marinade and sauté. Add the marinade to the chicken.
3. Bring to a boil and simmer till sauce is slightly reduced and thickened. Stir occasionally.
4. Adjust to taste and add more water if necessary.

FRIED RICE

"Chamorro fried rice is absolutely fulfilling!! It is a meal in itself, no need for extra meat! My favorite meat to use is chopped, left over bbq steak and chorizos espanot."

INGREDIENTS / DIRECTIONS

Set 1
4 c. cooked, long grain
   white rice

Set 2
½ onion, chopped
3 cloves garlic, minced
3 T. vegetable oil
1-2 c. chopped meat (bbq beef,
   spam, chorizos espanot etc.)

Set 3
1 c. vegetables
1/8 c. soy sauce
½ t. garlic powder
¼ t. black pepper
3 eggs, scrambled
2 T. butter
½ t. seasoning salt

Tools: large pot

1. Cook rice according to directions.
2. In large pot, sautee garlic and onions in 2 tablespoons oil. Add meat and sauté for 3 minutes.
3. Pour in vegetables (diced celery, carrots, corn, peas etc.) and sauté till softened.
4. Add rice, soy sauce, seasonings, scrambled eggs, and butter.
5. Fold mixture to combine all of the ingredients. Add more soy sauce, seasonings, butter or oil to taste.

SHRIMP IN COCONUT MILK

"Otherwise called kaddon uhang (kaw-don uw-hang), is an absolute favorite shrimp dish. Enriched with a coconut milk soup base, green beans and tomatoes, it is perfect with a bowl of hot, white rice. My mother-in-law sprinkles flour over the mix to make this dish wonderfully thick!"

INGREDIENTS / DIRECTIONS

Set 1
1 med. onion, chopped
1 ½ lbs. green beans, halved
   lengthwise and crosswise
4 T. butter
4 T. flour
2 c. hot water

Set 2
2 lbs. raw shrimp
   with shells on
1 ¾ t. salt
1 t. garlic powder

Set 3
1 - 13.5 oz can thick
   coconut milk
½ c. diced, canned
   tomatoes

Tools: *large pot*

1. Using a large pot, sauté onions and beans in butter.
2. Sprinkle flour into pot. Stir quickly. Immediately add hot water and continue to stir.
3. Mix salt and pepper together.
4. Add shrimp, salt, and garlic powder. Cook till shrimp is pink and mixture is bubbly.
5. Add coconut milk and diced tomatoes; stir to combine.
6. Reduce to a lower heat and cook for 10 more minutes.

SIOPAO

"Siopao, a Filipino specialty, is just one of those things! This steamed bread is filled with chicken, pork or beef in a savory sauce. This is also great with chicken kelaguen. Here is my mother-in-law's recipe."

INGREDIENTS / DIRECTIONS

DOUGH

Set 1	Set 2
3 – ¼ oz. pkgs. rapid rise yeast	3 ½ c. flour
1 ¼ c. warm water	
3 T. oil	
2/3 c. + 2 T. sugar	
1 t. salt	

Tools: large bowl, kitchen towel, wax paper, steamer

1. Cut wax paper into 4x4 pieces. Set aside.
2. Pour warm water into large bowl.
3. Sprinkle yeast over the water. Let set for a few minutes then stir to dissolve.
4. Add oil, sugar and salt. Stir.
5. Incorporate 2 cups of the flour and gradually add more flour to form a soft, slightly sticky dough. You will probably use all of the 3 ½ cups. DO NOT ADD ANY MORE. Dough will be sticky, but that is fine.
6. Knead soft dough a few minutes.
7. Let rise to double in size, about 1 hour.
8. Punch down and let rise to double in size again, about an hour.
9. Tear balls of dough into 12 equal portions and pat it out one at a time. Do not use a rolling pin! The dough should be thicker, slight "mound" in the middle (top of the

cooked siopao), and thinner on the edges (where it will be gathered and tucked on the bottom, yielding enough dough on the bottom).

10. Place about two small spoons of filling in the center of dough. Do not be tempted to add more as it may cause the dough to be too thin and tear.

11. Gather edges and twist to seal.

12. Place that seam on a piece of wax paper.

13. Set siopao in warm, draft free area and allow to rise, about 40 minutes.

14. Set up steamer and lay siopao, about 2 inch space between each. Set a kitchen towel between the steamer basket and the cover before covering!! This keeps the water from dripping on to siopao.

15. Steam for 18-20 minutes (varies according to size).

FILLING

Set 1
18 pieces cooked, shredded, skinless,
   boneless chicken thighs
1 c. chopped onion
1 T. vegetable oil
½ c. Mr. Yoshida's sauce
4 t. dark brown sugar
¼ t. black pepper
¼ t. garlic powder

Set 2
2 t. dark brown sugar
1 t. Mr. Yoshida's
   sauce

****This will yield enough filling for 3-4 batches of the siopao dough.****

Tools: *large pot, medium container*

1. Sautee onions in large pot using vegetable oil. Add chicken and stir till cooked.

2. Pour ½ c. of Mr. Yoshida's sauce into the pot and add the 2 tablespoons of brown sugar, black pepper, and garlic powder.

3. Cook till liquid is reduced. Drain excess liquid. Season with more sugar and sauce if desired.
4. Cool in fridge.
5. Chop cooked chicken more finely. Drain any remaining liquid before filling the dough.

HELPFUL HINT

Leftover chopped chicken, pork or beef may also be used.

SPAM JAM

"My children love this concoction of spam, corn, and tomato sauce! Many non-islanders balk at the thought of spam. Frankly, not only do we favor this canned meat, it is quite a delicacy for us!! You can even find it on the menus of McDonalds restaurants throughout Guam."

INGREDIENTS / INSTRUCTIONS

Set 1
¼ c. chopped onions (opt.)
4 cloves garlic, minced

Set 2
2 cans reduced sodium spam

Set 3
30 oz. can of tomato
   sauce
1 – 15 oz. can of
   sweet corn
½ t. garlic powder
¼ t. black pepper

Tools: *large pot*

1. Sautee onions and garlic in large pot. Add spam and sauté. Add tomato sauce and corn.

Try substituting the corn for sweet peas or green beans. Alternatively, add the peas and / or beans in addition to the corn.

GUAM DESSERTS

Yummy for the tummy

AHU

(aw-who)

"This is absolutely comforting after a long, stressful day!!!!! Per my grandma Cabe, let ahu come to room temperature before placing it in the fridge. This will keep the ahu thick."

INGREDIENTS / DIRECTIONS

Set 1	Set 2	Set 3
2 c. ahu meat, shredded	12 c. water	1 T. cornstarch
1 ½ - 2 c. tapioca starch	1 ½ c. sugar	1 T. water

Tools*: medium bowl, large pot*

1. Mix ahu meat with 1 ½ cups tapioca starch. If necessary, add a little bit of water to form an easy to stir paste.
2. Pour 12 cups water and 1 ½ cups sugar into a large pot. Bring to a boil.
3. Taste water and add more sugar if desired.
4. Pinch manha mixture and drop a small "ball" into the boiling water. Wait for 2-3 minutes and look to see if a gel forms around the manha pieces. If not, add about ½ cup tapioca starch to the bowl of manha/tapioca and stir, adding a little more water if necessary.
5. Continue to drop balls of manha/tapioca into the boiling water.
6. Let boil till mixture thickens, about 10-20 minutes. Stir constantly.
7. Ahu may be thickened more if desired: mix 1 tablespoon cornstarch and 1 tablespoon water. Pour into boiling ahu. Boil for two more minutes.
8. Eat and enjoy!!
9. Cover and let cool to room temperature before placing in the fridge.

I had made ahu during my early college years. It always thinned out the next day!! My grandma told me not to put it in the fridge till it cooled down. Walla!! I made ahu and it lasted for five nights in the fridge. It was quite thick the first two days, and just a bit thinner subsequent days. However, it was not runny like it was years ago, and was soooo delicious!

BANANA LUMPIA

(lewm-pia)

"This is delicious!! You can only use the Filipino lumpia (springroll) wrapper because it is paper-thin. The next time I make these, I will add some coconut candy with the plantain. How about some vanilla ice-cream on the side? Imagine: hot, crispy, sweet banana, with caramel coconut and vanilla ice-cream……"

INGREDIENTS / DIRECTIONS

Set 1	Set 2	Set 3
6 plantains	sugar	oil for deep frying
1 box of lumpia wrappers	small bowl of water	

***Tools**: cookie sheet, wax paper, large fry pan, pastry brush*

1. Slice each plantain in half cross wise then length wise, yielding four long slices. Peel the skin off (easiest to cut with the skin on).
2. Separate the lumpia wrappers. These are very delicate, a few may tear.
3. Put ½ t. of sugar 1 inch from the edge of the wrapper nearest to you. Spread the sugar within 2-3 inches, left to right. Place a slice of the plantain on top of the sugar. Sprinkle another ½ t of sugar over the plantain. Fold the edge nearest you over the plantain and wrap burrito style. Before completely wrapping, brush a little bit of water over the open edge to seal.
4. Lay lumpia on a cookie sheet allowing water seal to dry.
5. Store and freeze in a freezer bag layered with wax paper.
6. For best results, deep fry lumpia while it is frozen.

BUCHI BUCHI

(bu-chee bu-chee)

"My baked turnovers are good, but this fried version, it is even better. The key to this dessert is a good dough. One Summer at home, my best friend Melonie Quintanilla and I used the baked dough to make buchi buchi. That did not turn out well because it had too much Crisco. Now, I have come up with a great recipe reminiscent of the good old days."

INGREDIENTS / DIRECTIONS

FILLING

<u>Set 1</u>
3 - 15 oz. cans pureed pumpkin
1 t. cinnamon
¼ t. pumpkin pie spice
¼ t. vanilla
¼ c. white sugar
1½ c. dark brown sugar

Tools: *colander, medium bowl, large pot*

1. Fresh pureed pumpkin is best, if none is available canned is ok. Place pumpkin in colander, set into a bowl, and let drain overnight in the fridge.

2. Place pumpkin in large pot, over medium heat. Add sugars and spices. Adjust brown sugar and seasonings to taste. Stir, heating only to melt sugar. Cool completely!

PASTRY

Set 1	Set 2	Set 3
4 c. flour	½ c. Crisco	1 – 13.5 oz can
½ c. sugar		coconut milk, cold

Tools: *large bowl, rolling pin, 4-5 inch pot cover, wax paper, large pot, oil*

1. Combine flour and sugar. Cut the shortening in and incorporate till mixture resembles course crumbs.
2. Slowly add cold coconut milk along the edge of the bowl while gently folding the crumbs over itself. Fold the crumbs till it becomes a non-sticky mass. DO NOT KNEAD THE DOUGH!!!! [A]
3. Divide dough. Roll out onto lightly floured surface, 1/8 inch thick.
4. Cut with pot cover, about 5 in. diameter, no larger. Fill with 2-3 T. of filling on one half of pastry. Fold the other half of dough over filling, seal the edges with a fork. [B]
5. Lay buchi buchi in a single layer on a dry cookie sheet, let harden in the freezer. To store buchi buchi, layer in a covered container, separated by wax paper.
6. When ready to cook, prepare deep fryer. Fry buchi buchi while frozen on medium to medium-high heat.
7. Cool on paper towel lined colander and enjoy!!

HELPFUL HINTS

    A. Pour the coconut milk along the edge of the bowl while fingers incorporate the milk into the dry mix. Handle the dough to combine the mixture without kneading. This will result in a tender pastry!!

    B. Experiment with the first pastry to put as much filling onto the dough, leaving enough room to close the pastry over the filling and seal with a fork.

CASSAVA CAKE

"Growing up I loved the sweet manha tamales. Well, since I have had my Nina's cassava cake, tamales no more!! It is absolutely scrumptious and she is gladly sharing this recipe with us!!"

INGREDIENTS / DIRECTIONS

<u>Set 1</u>
4 – 16 oz. pkgs. grated cassava
3 – 12 oz. jars macapuno STRIPS (do not use cubes etc.)
6 eggs
2 – 13.5 oz. cans coconut milk
2 – 12 oz. cans carnation milk
1 stick butter, melted
1 ½ c. sugar

Tools: large bowl, large baking pan, about 2-3 inches deep

Preheat oven to 350 degrees.

1. Combine all ingredients in a large bowl. Mix thoroughly.
2. Pour into baking pan.
3. Bake for 1 to 1 ½ hours or till golden brown.

CHAMPULADO

(cham-poo-law-do)

"This is an old time favorite. It is hot, chocolate rice pudding....though some like it cold."

INGREDIENTS / DIRECTIONS

Set 1
1 ½ c. uncooked, Calrose rice
14 c. water

Set 2
1/3 c. unsweetened cocoa powder,
    sifted
2 c. water

Set 3
2 c. 2 % milk, warm
1 ½ c. sugar

Set 4
2 T. cornstarch
2 T. water

Tools: large pot, 4 cup measuring pitcher

1. Pour 8 cups of the water into a large pot. Add the 1 ½ cups of raw rice. Bring to a boil. Stir often to avoid burning at the bottom. Lower heat and continue to boil.

2. Mix cornstarch and 2 tablespoons water in a small cup. Set aside.

3. As #1 boils, water will evaporate. After about 20 minutes of boiling, add 6 more cups of water. Stir often and boil for 10 minutes.

4. Mix the cocoa powder and 2 cups of water in the pitcher. Pour into pot.

5. Let boil another 25 minutes. Add 1 ½ cups sugar.

6. Pour in the warm milk. Stir, taste, and add more sugar if desired. Bring to a gentle boil.

7. Add the cornstarch mixture to the pot and cook another two minutes.

COCONUT CREAM PIE

"On Guam, there are favorite bakeries along the roadside where you can pick-up a box or two of delicious pie. However, there is nothing like homemade pie, any flavor. If you like coconut, here is truly the best coconut cream pie, concocted by me. You really do have to use freshly grated coconut, no preserved/processed stuff for this recipe!! I developed this especially for my stint as coordinator for one of the Guam Liberation celebrations in Germany."

INGREDIENTS / DIRECTIONS

FILLING

Set 1	Set 2	Set 3
4 egg yolks	2 ½ c. 2% milk	½ stick of butter
½ c. sugar		1 ½ c. fresh, grated
½ c. cornstarch		coconut
1/8 t. salt		1 t. vanilla

Set 4
¼ c. fresh, grated coconut, for decor

Tools: *medium pot, whisk*

1. Combine egg yolks, sugar, cornstarch, and salt in a medium pot. Mix thoroughly.
2. Whisk in the milk and cook over medium heat. Stir constantly until the mix thickens, about 10-15 minutes. Ignore the lumps. It will disappear as custard thickens. Lower the heat to low and cook custard until it is quite thick.
3. Remove completely from the heat, add the butter, stir until it melts. Add the coconut and stir to combine. Pour into a bowl and set aside to cool.

CRUST

1. Thaw 9 or 10 in. pie crust. Bake as directed on the package. Keep the oven on for the garnish.

GARNISH

1. Spread ¼ cup coconut on a cookie sheet and toast till golden brown. Set aside.

MERINGUE

Set 1	Set 2	Set 3
5 egg whites	pinch of salt	½ c. sugar
	½ t. cream of tartar	1 t. vanilla

Tools*: large stainless steel bowl, small pot, electric beater*

1. Put egg whites in bowl and place over a pot of gently simmering water until warm. Remove from heat.
2. Beat egg whites until foamy.
3. Add salt and cream of tartar and continue to beat till soft white peaks form. Add sugar, 1 tablespoon at a time, beating well after each addition. Add vanilla and beat until stiff, glossy peaks form. [A]
4. Pour filling into pie crust.
5. Spread the meringue over the filling. Make sure to spread the meringue to the inside edges of the crust.
6. Swirl the top decoratively with a spoon or a spatula. Sprinkle toasted coconut. Bake till lightly browned on top, about 10 minutes.
7. Place pie in a draft free area that is not too cold and let cool.

HELPFUL HINTS

A. Egg whites can be beaten until soft or stiff peaks form. The egg whites start out with a transparent color. As they are beaten, they transform into a white color and it is at this point that they will take on the soft / stiff characteristics. Egg whites are at the soft peak stage when the tip of the whites fall over as the beaters are removed. The stiff peak stage is when the egg whites maintain a point and do not fall over. Do not over beat as the egg whites will separate and become curdled.

CUSTARD PIE

"My favorite pie, since forever ago, has always been custard pie. Coupled with a great crust, you have a winner."

INGREDIENTS / DIRECTIONS

<u>Set 1</u>
9 in. deep dish pie crust

<u>Set 2</u>
5 whole eggs, room temp.
½ c. + 2 T. sugar
½ t. vanilla
½ t. almond extract

<u>Set 3</u>
2 ½ c. scalded
    evaporated milk

<u>Set 4</u>
nutmeg for dusting

Tools: *medium bowl, whisk, cookie sheet*

Preheat oven to 400 degrees with the cookie sheet in the oven.

1. Thaw the pie crust.
2. In a medium bowl, whisk the eggs, sugar, vanilla and almond extract.
3. Slowly whisk ¼ c. of scalded milk into the egg mixture. Continue this process until all of the milk has been added to the egg mixture.
4. Pierce the pie crust.
5. Place the pie crust on top of the cookie sheet.
6. Pour custard in.
7. Sprinkle the nutmeg over the custard (preferably freshly grated).
8. Bake for 15 minutes then reduce heat to 375 degrees for another 40 to 50 min. or till the toothpick inserted in center comes out clean. Cool on rack for 30 min. then chill in fridge.

GUYURIA

(gew-dzu-ree-ya)

"My mom came up with this recipe. I remember when we would spend the day making guyuria for family and friends. I have yet to find a better tasting guyuria! These used to be called Chamorro jawbreakers because they were so hard.....made without butter. With the addition of butter, it produces the best guyuria ever!

INGREDIENTS / DIRECTIONS

DOUGH

Set 1   Set 2
5 lb. bag all-purpose flour   4 – 13.5 oz. cans coconut milk
1 stick unsalted butter, softened

Tools*: large bowl, large pot, slotted ladle, colander, large cake pan, small pot*

1. Pour the entire bag of flour into a large bowl.
2. Chop softened butter into the bowl of flour. Mix till resembles course crumbs.
3. Add enough coconut milk to form a soft, non-sticky dough.
4. Knead slightly.
5. Pinch off pieces of dough small enough to spread over the back of a fork.
6. Roll the dough off the back of the fork, pinching the edge of the dough with pointed ends of the fork.
7. Heat a large pot of oil medium to medium-high.
8. With a large slotted ladle, place rolled dough into the oil. LOAD THE LADLLE WITH DOUGH OVER THE COUNTER TOP NOT OVER THE POT OF OIL!!!!
9. Fry till golden brown and stir to cook evenly.

10. Adjust heat such that guyuria cooks inside before getting burnt on the outside.

11. Each batch takes about 25 to 30 minutes to cook properly.

12. Remove the first batch and drain in a colander.

13. Repeat till all are cooked

SYRUP

<u>Set 1</u>
lots of sugar
1 c. water

1. In a small pot, heat water on medium.
2. Add enough sugar to form a very thick syrup.
3. Place pot in the fridge till cooled. Add more sugar to form a grainy syrup.
4. Pour just a little bit of syrup over the guyuria and stir. Pour only enough syrup so as not to leave a layer of syrup on the bottom of the pan.
5. Let dry for one hour. Sprinkle some dry sugar and add some syrup as well. Stir.
6. Allow to dry after each addition of syrup.
7. The guyuria is great with a moderate amount of sugar.
8. Store in an air tight container or in freezer bags.

LATIYA

(la-ti-dza)

"Yummmm, this is my absolute favorite Chamorro dessert!! I have yet to try a latiya that is as good as my recipe...just my opinion. The combination of the Betty Crocker pound cake and this custard is scrumptious!"

INGREDIENTS / DIRECTIONS

CAKE

Set 1
Betty Crocker boxed pound cake mix

Tools*: medium bowl, electric beater*

1. Bake cake as directed on box. Cool. Slice ½ inch thick.
2. If the boxed pound cake mix is not available, Sara Lee Pound Cake in the freezer section will be fine. Defrost then slice. Arrange slices in a tray that has a 2 inch lip.

CUSTARD

Set 1	Set 2	Set 3
2 – 12 oz. cans evaporated milk	6 eggs	½ c. cornstarch
2 cans water	4 t. vanilla	2/3 c. water
1 stick butter		
1 c. sugar		

Set 4
cinnamon for dusting

Tools: *large pot, whisk, electric beater, medium bowl, small bowl, containers with 2 inch lip,*

1. Pour milk into pot over medium high heat. Refill the two cans with water and pour into the pot. Add butter and sugar. Stir occasionally, and bring to a gentle boil.

2. While waiting for #1 to boil, in a medium bowl beat the eggs and vanilla. Set aside.

3. In a small bowl, mix the cornstarch and water.

4. When #1 reaches a gentle boil, slowly pour in the eggs/vanilla as you quickly whisk the mixture in the pot. Ignore the shreds of eggs as this will not be evident in the final taste and texture. Stir constantly. Let this come to a gentle boil then add the cornstarch mixture. Stir and cook for two minutes.

5. Pour custard over cake and sprinkle with cinnamon. Cool uncovered in the fridge.

6. This is best the next day!!

There are many variations on latiya. Some folks use sponge cake instead of pound. The custard may or may not use eggs.

LECHE FLAN

(le-tsee flan)

"If you like thick custard, this is it. It uses whole eggs, vs. egg yolks, so it is not as rich as flan made with egg yolks only. However, this is a great custard!!"

INGREDIENTS / DIRECTIONS

CARAMEL

<u>Set 1</u>
1 c. sugar
¼ c. water

Tools: small pot,   8x8 metal / glass dish,   large enough pan for a hot water bath

1. Caramelize 1 cup of the sugar in a pot on medium heat. Stir constantly. When browned, stand back while adding ¼ cup water and stirring constantly. Lower heat and stir for 1 minute to form a caramel mixture. Pour into the 8 x 8 dish. Set aside.

FLAN

<u>Set 1</u>   <u>Set 2</u>
9 large eggs   2 – 12 oz. cans evaporated milk
~. sugar   1 c. 2% milk
salt   4 t. vanilla

medium bowl,   whisk

to 350 degrees.

1. Lightly beat together the eggs, sugar and salt in the medium bowl. Add the milk and vanilla. Set aside.
2. Make a water bath by placing the large pan on the oven rack. Put 8 x 8 into the pan. Carefully pour water into the larger pan, trying not to get water into the 8 x 8 dish.
3. Pour custard into 8 x 8 (do not overfill), gently push rack in and close the oven door.
4. Bake 35 min. or till toothpick inserted in center comes out clean.
5. Let flan cool 15 minutes. Run knife along sides of dish to loosen.
6. Put a platter over dish and invert gently. Refrigerate till ready to serve.

NAN CHONG'S COOKIES

"These are old fashioned, delicious cookies. They are unusual, wonderful, and I just can not get enough of them! This is a recipe from my Nina (Auntie Daling). It was given to her by her aunt, and I am thrilled that Nina has shared this with us."

INGREDIENTS / DIRECTIONS

Set 1
5 c. flour
1 ¼ t. baking powder
½ t. baking soda

Set 2
3 eggs
2 sticks butter
1 c. shortening
1 ¼ c. sugar
1 ¼ t. vanilla
½ t. lemon extract

Tools: large plastic bowl,   medium bowl,   electric beater,   non stick cookie sheets or paper

Preheat oven to 350 degrees.

1. Combine all of set 1 into a medium bowl. Stir and set aside.
2. Beat butter and Crisco till well combined. Add eggs, extracts, and sugar. Beat thoroughly.
3. Pour dry ingredients into wet ingredients and combine with one hand to form a soft dough.
4. Pinch off dough and roll to make a 1.5 inch log between your palms. Flatten slightly in hands. Lay on cookie sheet. Use fork to press and flatten slightly.
5. Bake till golden brown, about 23 minutes. Cool on wire rack.

PUMPKIN PASTIT

(pus-tit)

"You can use pumpkin, apple or papaya as a filling for this pastit. This is the best recipe I have come across, developed by yours truly. Make some space in the freezer to lay a cookie sheet in such that you can freeze pastit prior to storing."

INGREDIENTS / DIRECTIONS

FILLING

<u>Set 1</u>
3 – 15 oz. cans pureed pumpkin
1 ½ c. dark brown sugar
¼ c. white sugar
1 t. cinnamon
¼ t. pumpkin spice
¼ t. vanilla

***Tools**: colander, medium bowl, large pot*

1. Fresh pureed pumpkin is best, if none is available canned is ok. Place pumpkin in colander, set into a bowl, and let drain overnight in the fridge.
2. Place pumpkin in large pot, over medium heat. Add sugars and spices. Adjust brown sugar and seasonings to taste. Stir, heating only to melt sugar. Cool completely!

BAKED PASTRY

<u>Set 1</u>	<u>Set 2</u>	<u>Set 3</u>
5 c. flour	1 c. white shortening	2-3 c. ice water
½ c. sugar		

Tools*: large bowl, rolling pin, 4-5 inch pot cover, non-stick cookie sheets, wax paper*

1. Combine flour and sugar. Cut the shortening in and incorporate till mixture resembles course crumbs.

2. Slowly add ice water along the edge of the bowl while gently folding the crumbs over itself. Fold the dough till it becomes a non-sticky mass. DO NOT KNEAD THE DOUGH!!!! **A**

3. Divide dough. Roll out onto lightly floured surface, 1/8 inch thick.

4. Cut with pot cover, about 5 in. diameter, no larger. Fill with 3-4 T. of filling on one half of pastry. Fold the other half of dough over filling, seal the edges with a fork. **B**

5. Puncture top of pastry with tines of fork, three times, evenly spaced (this allows steam to escape while pastit is baking.)

6. Lay pastit in a single layer on a dry cookie sheet, let harden in the freezer. To store pastit, layer in a covered container, separated by wax paper.

7. When ready to bake, **preheat oven to 350 degrees**, brush frozen pastit with egg wash (DO NOT THAW), and bake till nicely browned, approx. 45 minutes. The steam holes may need to be pierced again after 20 minutes of baking.

8. Cool on a wire rack and enjoy!!

EGG WASH

Set 1
2 egg yolks
½ t. sugar
2 T. whole milk

Tools*: small bowl, pastry brush*

1. Combine all of the above till sugar is dissolved. Brush over frozen pastit, ensuring there is no excess egg wash sitting on edges of pastry.

HELPFUL HINTS

A. Pour the ice water along the edge of the bowl while fingers incorporate the water into the dry mix. Handle the dough to combine the mixture without kneading. This will result in a tender pastry!!

B. Experiment with the first pastit to put as much filling onto the dough, leaving enough room to close the pastry over the filling and seal with a fork.

Please be generous with the filling and keep the dough to no more than an 1/8 inch thick. On my last trip to Guam in Feb 2006, I was very disappointed to bite into an apple pastit and a buchi buchi……a mouthful of dough and very little of the delicious fillings!

ROSKETTE

"I have not had better roskette than this! This is one of my previously guarded secrets!!
It's great in miniature form, the flattened dough no bigger than a nickel."

INGREDIENTS / DIRECTIONS

Set 1
2 c. flour
1 – 16 oz. box cornstarch
1 t. baking powder

Set 2
1 ½ c. sugar
1 c. butter
2 eggs
1 t. vanilla

Set 3
1 c. heavy cream

Tools: medium bowl, large bowl, electric beater, non-stick baking paper, 2 cookie sheets

Preheat oven to 350 degrees.

1. In a medium bowl, combine flour, cornstarch and baking powder.
2. Cream butter and sugar in a large bowl.
3. Beat into #2 the eggs and vanilla till well combined.
4. Add dry ingredients to the creamed mixture and combine with hands.
5. Pour ¾ cup of cream into mixture, at first, to form a soft, slightly sticky dough. Add remaining cream if necessary.
6. Form into balls less than an inch in diameter.
7. Place balls on cookie sheets.
8. Dip tines of fork into flour and press crisscross onto balls.
9. Bake for 20-25 minutes till edges are brown.

VELVET CAKE

"There is just something about a great velvet cake with cream cheese frosting! This recipe I came up with is absolutely delicious even without the homemade topping!!

INGREDIENTS / DIRECTIONS

CAKE

Set 1
2 c. flour, measured then sifted
2 T. unsweetened cocoa powder,
  sifted
1 ½ t. baking soda
1 t. salt

Set 2
2 sticks butter, room temp.
1 ¾ c. sugar
2 t. vanilla
3 eggs, room temp
red food coloring

Set 3
1 c. buttermilk
2 T. vinegar

Tools: *Bundt pan,   non-stick spray,   medium bowl,   large bowl,   electric beater*

Preheat oven to 350 degrees.

1. Spray the Bundt pan with non-stick spray.
2. In a medium bowl, combine dry ingredients and set aside. Remember to sift the flour and cocoa powder.
3. Cream butter and sugar in a large bowl. Add vanilla, eggs and food coloring.
4. Combine buttermilk and vinegar.
5. Pour half of dry ingredients then half of the buttermilk/vinegar into #3. Beat till barely combined then add remaining dry ingredients and liquids. Beat till well combined.
6. Pour batter into pan and bake about 40 minutes or till toothpick inserted in center comes out clean. Cool on wire rack for 10 min. Remove from pan and cool.

FROSTING

<u>Set 1</u>
1 stick butter, room temperature
2-8 oz. blocks of cream cheese, room temperature
enough sifted powdered sugar to desired sweetness

Tools*: medium bowl, strainer, electric beater*

1. Beat butter till light and fluffy. Add cream cheese and beat till well combined.
2. Add enough sifted powdered sugar to desired sweetness
3. Spread and fluff frosting over cooled cake.

This is wonderfully delicious the next day!!

MIX OF AMERICA

Fare from a mix of cultures found in the USA

BAGOGI

(ba-go-gee)

"My husband's favorite dish while in Korea was bagogi. It is still one he loves and I happen to like it too. Recipe courtesy of Nancy White."

INGREDIENTS / DIRECTIONS

Set 1
2 lbs. top sirloin

Set 2
1 medium onion, thinly sliced
16 T. soy sauce
½ t. black pepper
9 T. brown sugar
10 cloves garlic, minced

Set 2 cont.
2 T. minced ginger
2 t. sesame oil
6 T. Coke

Set 3
1 T. vegetable oil
1 medium onion, thinly sliced

Set 4
sesame seeds for garnish

Tools: large bowl, medium bowl, large pot

1. Rinse the meat. Cut the beef into very thin slices, about 2 inches long and place in a medium bowl. It is essential to this recipe that the slices are about 1/8 inch thick. Set aside. [A]

2. In a large bowl, combine half of the sliced onions, soy sauce, black pepper, 9 tablespoons brown sugar, garlic, ginger, sesame oil, coke or apple juice. Stir to combine. Taste mixture, add more sugar if necessary.

3. Add meat to the mixture and let marinate for 30 minutes, no more than an hour.

4. Heat pot and 1 tablespoon of vegetable oil. Sautee remaining onions, add beef and onions from the marinade.

5. Pour ½ of marinade into the meat and simmer uncovered to slightly reduce liquid.
6. Use less marinade if a stir-fried bagogi is preferred.

BEEF STEW

"Years ago, I finally came up with a beef stew recipe that is quite comforting."

INGREDIENTS / DIRECTIONS

Set 1
2 lbs. beef stew meat
½ t. salt
½ t. pepper
2 T. vegetable oil

Set 2
1 potato, peeled, cubed
28 oz. beef broth
4 carrots, sliced
¼ t. rosemary
¼ t. ground thyme
1 t. Dijon mustard
pinch of curry powder
½ can of diced tomatoes
2 stalks celery, sliced

Set 3
2 T. cornstarch
mixed with
1 T. water

Tools: medium bowl,   large pot

1. Place meat, salt, and pepper in a bowl. Toss to coat.
2. Heat oil in large pot over medium. Add meat and brown.
3. Add broth, tomatoes, and seasonings. Bring to a boil. Lower heat, cover and simmer for 45 minutes or until beef is tender. Add carrots, celery, and potatoes. Cook till tender.
4. Pour cornstarch mixture into simmering beef stew to thicken. Cook 2 more minutes.

CHEESY BURGER

"The blue cheese really lends a delightful surprise to these burgers. I make a whole batch of patties and freeze them, ready to cook as needed."

INGREDIENTS / DIRECTIONS

Set 1
½ c. crumbled blue cheese
3 lbs. lean ground beef
½ c. fresh chives
½ c. diced onions
½ t. Tabasco

Set 1 cont.
2 t. Worcestershire sauce
2 t. black pepper
3 t. salt
2 t. dry mustard

Tools: *large bowl*

1. In a large bowl, combine all ingredients and mix thoroughly.
2. Cover and place in fridge for at least 2 hours.
3. Form into patties and grill.
4. If freezing, place each patty between two sheets of deli paper, then put it in a fold-top sandwich bag. Seal in a freezer bag.

CHILI

"This is a great, thick chili. It leans on the slightly sweet & quite savory side as opposed to tomato saucy. The color and taste come from the beer, coffee and cocoa powder."

INGREDIENTS / DIRECTIONS

<u>Set 1</u>
3 lbs. lean, ground turkey

<u>Set 2</u>
2 onions, diced
5 cloves garlic, minced
14 oz. can diced tomatoes
14 oz. can beef broth
2-6 oz. cans tomato paste
3 – 15 oz. cans kidney beans
12 oz. can / bottle dark beer
1 c. strong coffee

<u>Set 3</u>
1 T. unsweetened
   cocoa powder
¼ c. brown sugar
4 T. chili powder
¾ T. ground cumin
1 ½ t. coriander
2 t. dried oregano
1 t. salt

Tools: colander, large pot

1. Open cans of beans. Drain and rinse.
2. Brown the ground turkey (drain liquid if preferred). Add in the garlic and onions, cook for 5 minutes. Add all ingredients and stir.
3. Bring to a boil then simmer for 1 hour.
4. Adjust seasonings to taste.

CORN BREAD

"This is a great corn bread by accident! I put in too much butter, but it was for the best."

INGREDIENTS / DIRECTIONS

Set 1
1/3 c. white sugar
1/3 c. light brown sugar
1 t. salt
1 stick butter, softened
1 t. vanilla
2 eggs

Set 2
2 c. all-purpose flour
1 T. baking powder
¾ c. cornmeal

Set 3
1 1/3 c. whole milk

Tools: medium bowl, large bowl, electric beater, 8 x 8 or muffin pan

Preheat oven to 400 degrees.

1. In a medium bowl, combine flour, baking powder and cornmeal.
2. Beat together sugar, salt, butter and vanilla in a large bowl. Beat in eggs one at a time, beat well after each.
3. Pour half of #1 and half of the milk into #2; beat. Stir. Add remaining flour and milk. Beat till well combined.
4. Pour into the 8 x 8 pan or into paper muffin cups.
5. Bake for 40 minutes or till a toothpick inserted in the center comes out clean.

GUMBO

"My kids love this, especially with lots of sausage."

INGREDIENTS / DIRECTIONS

Set 1
¾ c. all purpose flour

Set 2
1 ½ - 2 lbs. low-fat smoked
   sausage, sliced ¼ in. thick
1 ½ - 2 lbs. chicken tenderloins,
   sliced ¼ in. thick

Set 3
1 med. onion, diced
5 cloves garlic,
   minced
1 ½ c. sliced celery
1 small, green, bell
   pepper, diced

Set 4
6 c. hot water
2 c. low sodium chicken broth

Set 5
2 T. Worcestershire
½ t. dried thyme
½ t. Cajun seasoning

Set 5 cont.
2 bay leaves
salt & pepper

Tools: 9 x 13 cookie sheet w/lip,   non-stick spray,   large pot

Preheat oven to 400 degrees.

1. Pour flour into the cookie pan, put in oven and brown for 15-20 minutes. Stir every few minutes.
2. Spray large pot with non-stick spray and sautee sausage. Remove sausage.
3. In same pot, brown the chicken, drain any liquids and set chicken aside.
4. Wipe the pot and spray with non-stick spray. Sautee onions and garlic. Add celery, bell pepper and cook to soften.
5. Sprinkle flour over veggies and stir. Gradually add in the water and broth, stirring constantly. Bring to a boil.
6. Add sausage, chicken and remaining dry ingredients and Worcestershire sauce. Bring to a boil. Reduce and simmer for 45 minutes.

MEATBALLS

"The nice thing about homemade meatballs is that they do not have so much fat in them!!"

INGREDIENTS / DIRECTIONS

Set 1
6 slc. wheat bread

Set 2
2 lbs. lean, ground turkey
1 lb. lean, ground beef
4 cloves garlic, minced
½ c. finely diced onion
3 t. salt
3 t. black pepper
6 t. Worcestershire sauce

Set 3
60 oz. beef stock

Tools: *medium bowl, large bowl, large pot, large slotted scoop*

1. Soak bread in medium bowl of water for 10 minutes. Squeeze bread to drain the water.
2. In a large bowl, combine the bread and all of set 2.
3. Fill large pot 2/3 full of stock and / or water. Set on medium high heat and bring to a boil.
4. Roll meat into 1 inch balls.[A] Boil meatballs in batches for 30 minutes. Remove with slotted scoop.
5. Simmer in desired sauce in a crock pot for 30 minutes. [B]

HELPFUL HINTS

A. To do a taste test, roll a tiny ball of meat and simmer for 10 minutes. Adjust seasonings accordingly.
B. May also just dip meatballs in favorite sauce after cooking.

The meatballs can be frozen in a plastic container filled with broth.

MEATLOAF

"I love meatloaf every now and then. Here is a recipe I have used for almost 10 years."

INGREDIENTS / DIRECTIONS

MEATLOAF

Set 1
2 lbs. lean, ground beef
1 c. Italian style bread crumbs
2 eggs
1 large onion, diced

Set 1 cont.
3 t. salt
¾ c. ketchup
1 T. molasses

Tools: *large bowl,   9x13 baking dish sprayed with non-stick spray*

Preheat oven to 350 degrees.

1. Combine all ingredients.
2. Place into baking dish and shape into a flattened log.
3. Put in oven and bake for half an hour.
4. While waiting, prepare sauce.

SAUCE

Set 1
1 ¼ c. ketchup
¾ c. water
2 ½ T. molasses

Set 1 cont.
4 T. mustard
2 T. vinegar
2 ½ T. dark brown sugar

5. Mix all ingredients.
6. Remove meatloaf from the oven and punch holes.
7. Pour all of sauce over meatloaf and into pan.
8. Place back in oven and bake another one hour.

SCOTT'S SPAGHETTI

"This recipe is from my compadre Scott White. He simply makes the best pasta dishes!! One day in 1998 I decided to take notes while he made his spaghetti sauce from scratch. It has been the best sauce I have ever had."

INGREDIENTS / DIRECTIONS

Set 1
1 lb. ground beef
2 T. olive oil

Set 2
3 large cans of tomato sauce

Set 3
4 cloves garlic,
    minced
1 large onion,
    chopped

Set 4
1 can diced tomatoes,
    Primavera
1 can diced tomatoes,
    Spicy Pepper
1 large can crushed tomatoes
2 cans small tomato sauce

Set 4 cont.
1 T. basil
1 T. oregano
1 t. seasoned pepper blend
1 ½ to 2 T. sugar
dash of salt
dash of red pepper (opt.)

Tools: *large sauté pan,   large pot*

1. Brown beef in olive oil in sauté pan
2. Add onions and garlic.
3. Pour all of the tomato sauce into a large pot. Heat on medium-med. high.
4. Add the primavera and spicy pepper diced tomatoes.
5. Place browned beef into large pot.
6. Sprinkle in basil, oregano, pepper flakes, pepper blend, salt and sugar.

7. Cover and let simmer for 3 hours, stirring occasionally.
8. Alternatively, use a crock pot in place of the large pot and let simmer for 8 hours on low heat.

SPAGHETTI

"This is not a recipe from scratch. However, it yields a quick, flavorful and inexpensive meal."

INGREDIENTS / DIRECTIONS

SAUCE

Set 1	Set 2
2 lbs. lean, ground turkey	1 large can Del Monte spaghetti sauce, Garlic and Onion
	1 large can Del Monte spaghetti sauce, Mushroom

Tools*: large pot*

1. Brown turkey in large pot. Drain.
2. Add spaghetti sauce. Bring to gentle boil. Reduce heat and simmer for 30 minutes.
3. This freezes well. Cool in the fridge first. Freeze in plastic containers or freezer bags.

NOODLES

Set 1	Set 2	Set 3
water	1 lb. spaghetti noodles	parmesan cheese
½ t. salt		
1 T. vegetable oil		

Tools*: medium pot,   colander,   cheese grater*

1. Fill medium pot half full of water. Add salt and oil. Bring to a boil.

2. Add noodles and boil for only 5 minutes, just till al' dente. Drain.
3. Add meat sauce to the noodles.
4. Serve and sprinkle with freshly grated Parmesiano - Regiano cheese.

TURKEY BEAN SOUP

"The chili and curry powders both lend a great flavor to this soup."

INGREDIENTS / DIRECTIONS

Set 1
3-4 lbs. lean, ground turkey

Set 2
1 onion, diced
5 cloves garlic, minced
1 can diced tomatoes
45 oz. chicken broth
4 T. soy sauce
3 T. Worcestershire sauce
12 oz. can / bottle light beer
1 – 15.5 oz. can sweet corn
1 – 15.5 oz. can kidney beans
1 – 15.5 oz. can black beans
1 – 15.5 oz. can garbanzo beans
1 – 15.5 oz. can pinto beans

Set 2 cont.
3 ½ T. chili powder
2 T. curry powder
1 ½ t. dried thyme
2 t. dried oregano
1 t. dried parsley
¼ t. black pepper
1 ½ t. salt

Tools: colander, large pot

1. Drain and rinse the beans and corn.
2. Brown the turkey in a large pot. Drain liquid.
3. Add #1 and all other ingredients. Stir to combine.
4. Cover and bring to a boil. Reduce heat and simmer for 1 hour.

TREASURE CHEST
OF SWEETS

The author's collection of her
other favorite desserts

BANANA NUT BREAD

"Here is something fun in the making!! Banana nut bread with a twist: lots of chocolate chips, walnuts and spices. A great way to use those ripe bananas!"

INGREDIENTS / DIRECTIONS

Set 1
3 c. all purpose flour
1 ½ t. baking soda
1 ½ t. baking powder
½ t. ground cloves
½ t. ground cinnamon
½ t. ground all spice
½ t. ground nutmeg

Set 2
1 c. shortening
1 c. white sugar
1 c. brown sugar

Set 3
3 eggs

Set 4
1 ¼ c. buttermilk
3 large bananas, mashed
1 t. vanilla

Set 5
2 c. chopped walnuts
2 ½ c. semi-sweet chocolate chips

Tools: *electric beater, medium bowl, large bowl, 2-10 in. Bundt pans or 2-9x5 loaf pans, non-stick spray, rubber spatula*

Preheat oven to 350 degrees.

1. Stir together flour, baking soda, baking powder and spices in a medium bowl.
2. In large bowl, cream shortening and sugars. Add eggs one at a time, beating well after each addition. Beat in the buttermilk, bananas and vanilla. Add dry ingredients and beat till somewhat combined. Add chocolate chips and nuts, mixing with a rubber spatula till thoroughly combined.
3. Spray pans and pour in batter.
4. Bake for 60-70 minutes until a toothpick comes out clean.
5. Cool on a wire rack.

CAKE FROSTING

"My mom decorated cakes when I was growing up. She did an awesome job!! I dabbled a bit in cake decorating as a teenager, more in college, and finally had a home based cake decorating business in Germany. It was in Germany that I developed this recipe. If using a hand-held mixer, add 2 T. of Crisco and 1 T. of water to the recipe below."

INGREDIENTS / INSTRUCTIONS

Set 1
2 – 1 lb. boxes powdered sugar
½ t. cream of tartar
pinch of salt

Set 2
1 ¼ c. Crisco
½ c. + 1 T. water

Tools: *large bowl,   strainer,   electric beater*

1. Sift all dry ingredients into a large bowl.
2. Scoop Crisco into the dry ingredients and add all of the water.
3. Beat on low speed to combine, then on high till nice and fluffy.
4. Put frosting in a container. Place plastic wrap directly onto the surface of the frosting and against the container to seal. Let rest overnight to release air bubbles. Stir, do not beat, when ready to use.

This frosting may be frozen directly in the container. Thaw before use. Remove any hardened crystals (along edges). This frosting smoothes easily on a cake (remember to do a crumb coat first). To remove the icing from the cake board, allow it to dry then scrape off with a very thin, pointed, metal spatula.

CAKE DECORATING ICING

"This is great for piped decorations using cake decorating tips. If using a hand-held mixer, add 2 T. of Crisco and 1 T. of water to the recipe below."

INGREDIENTS / DIRECTIONS

Set 1
2 – 1 lb. boxes powdered sugar
½ t. cream of tartar
pinch of salt

Set 2
1 c. Crisco
½ c. water

Tools: large bowl,   strainer,   electric beater

1. In a large bowl, sift all ingredients together.
2. Add Crisco and water to #1.
3. Beat slowly at first, then on high speed till nice and fluffy.

This icing stores just like the cake frosting.

CHOCOLATE BISCOTTI

"A biscotti is akin to the Chamorro pantosta as both are dipped into coffee. Where as a biscotti is more like a crispy cookie, a pantosta is more like dried, sweet bread. Both are delicious with coffee!!"

INGREDIENTS / DIRECTIONS

DOUGH

Set 1
1 ¾ c. all purpose flour
1/3 c. unsweetened cocoa powder
2 t. baking powder

Set 2
1/3 c. butter
2/3 c. sugar

Set 3
2 eggs
1 ½ t. vanilla

Set 4
¾ c. semisweet chocolate chips
¼ c. chopped walnuts

Set 5
2 lbs. semisweet coating chocolate (Dove, Lindt
        or other high quality chocolate), chopped

Tools: medium bowl,   large bowl,   electric beater,   large cookie sheet,   wire cookie rack

EGG WASH

Set 1
1 beaten egg yolk
1 T. milk

Tools: small bowl,   pastry brush

Preheat oven to 375 degrees.

1. Combine flour, cocoa powder and baking powder in medium bowl. Set aside.
2. In large bowl, cream butter and sugar till combined. Beat in eggs and vanilla till combined.
3. Add #1 mix to #2. Using hands, combine the mixtures then add in chocolate pieces and walnuts.
4. Divide dough in half.
5. Lightly grease the cookie sheet. Shape each portion into a log, about 9 in. long x 2 in. wide x 1 in. high. On a cookie sheet, arrange logs 4 inches apart.
6. Combine the egg yolk and milk. Brush a thin layer of egg wash over each log.
7. Bake logs for 25 minutes. Cool on a cookie sheet for 30 minutes.
8. Cut each log diagonally into 1 centimeter thick slices. Place slices on a cookie sheet and bake in a 325 degrees oven for 15 minutes. Turn the slices over and bake another 10 to 15 minutes more till dry and crisp. Remove and cool on a wire rack.
9. Gently melt 2/3 of the coating chocolate till about 95 degrees. [A] Remove from the source of heat and gently fold in the remaining chocolate. Dip one side half way into chocolate and set on wire rack to dry. Makes about 30 slices.

HELPFUL HINTS

A. Chocolate pieces will retain shape when heated. Be careful not to overheat.

CHOCOLATE CHIP COOKIES

"This is a delicious recipe to have in your files. It yields a thick, soft cookie. When Auntie Bea Fabellano made her chocolate chip cookies, she used ¾ cup molasses instead of the corn syrup. Her version was great and it inspired this recipe, as my husband is not particularly fond of molasses. Myself, I prefer Auntie Bea's."

INGREDIENTS / DIRECTIONS

Set 1
2 ¼ c. flour
1 t. baking soda
1 t. salt

Set 2
1 c. butter Crisco
¾ c. corn syrup
¾ c. dark brown sugar
1 t. vanilla
2 eggs

Set 3
2 ½ c. semi-sweet
   chips

Tools: medium bowl,   large bowl,   cookie sheets,   non-stick baking paper

Preheat oven to 350 degrees.

1. Combine flour, baking soda, and salt in the medium bowl; set aside.
2. Cream Crisco, brown sugar, and corn syrup in the large bowl. Add in vanilla and eggs.
3. Pour the bowl of dry ingredients into the creamed mixture. Use one hand to mix thoroughly then add chocolate chips.
4. Place mounds of dough on non-stick paper (cookie scoop is helpful) about 2 inches apart.
5. Bake for 10-12 minutes or till browned on the bottom.

ENERGY BARS

"I met my good friend Lori Mendoza in college at the University of Oregon. One of the items in her care packages from home was the energy bars her grandma, Jo Rabago, made. These are sinfully delicious, and Lori is sharing it with us."

INGREDIENTS / DIRECTIONS

Set 1
2-10 oz. pkg. marshmallows
1 c. peanut butter
1 stick butter

Set 2
½ c. sesame seeds
6 c. rice krispies cereal
2 c. oats
1 c. peanuts
1 c. raisins

Tools: *9 x 13 pan,   additional baking pan,   non-stick spray*

Preheat oven to 350 degrees.

1. Spray 9 x 13 pan with non-stick spray.
2. Mix all of set 1 ingredients in a large pot over medium heat. Heat until melted.
3. Place all of set 2 ingredients into the additional baking pan and heat a few minutes in the oven
4. Pour the melted mixture over set 2 and mix to combine.
5. Spread into the 9 x 13 and allow to cool.
6. Cut into individual logs and wrap in wax paper.

POUND CAKE

"I love this pound cake.....the brown sugar gives this cake a beautiful color, excellent flavor and great texture. This is a cake wonderful on its own or with an accompaniment."

INGREDIENTS / DIRECTIONS

Set 1	Set 2	Set 3
3 c. all purpose flour, measured then sifted	1 stick butter	1 t. vanilla
¼ t. baking powder	2 c. dark brown sugar	6 eggs
½ t. salt	1 c. light brown sugar	
	8 oz. cream cheese, room temp.	

***Tools**: non-stick spray, medium bowl, large bowl, electric beater Bundt pan*

1. Spray the non-stick Bundt pan with non-stick spray. **Do not preheat the oven.**
2. Sift together the flour, baking powder and salt in a medium bowl.
3. In large bowl, beat the butter, sugar and cream cheese till light and fluffy. Beat in the vanilla and the eggs, one at a time, mixing completely after each addition.
4. Pour the #2 mixture into the #3 mixture and beat on low till combined.
5. Pour batter into the Bundt pan and place the cake in the oven. Set temperature to **350 degrees**. Bake for 70-80 minutes, a few minutes longer if necessary. Once done (toothpick test), turn off oven, leave cake in the oven for 15 minutes.
6. Remove from the oven and cool in the pan for 15 minutes. Turn over onto a wire rack to cool.

POUND CAKE II

"This is a delicious pound cake!"

INGREDIENTS / DIRECTIONS

Set 1
3 c. cake flour
½ t. salt
¼ t. baking soda

Set 2
1 ¼ c. unsalted butter
2 ½ c. white sugar
½ c. light brown sugar
6 eggs
1 t. vanilla

Set 3
1 c. sour cream

Tools: medium bowl, large bowl, electric beater, Bundt pan

Preheat oven to 350 degrees.

1. In a medium bowl, stir together flour, salt and baking soda. Set aside.
2. Cream butter and sugar in large bowl till light and fluffy. Add vanilla and beat in eggs one at a time.
3. Add sour cream and beat till combined.
4. Fold in flour. Pour into prepared pan.
5. Bake for 70 to 85 minutes or till toothpick inserted in center comes out clean.
6. Let cool in pan for 15 minutes then remove to cool on wire rack.

SANDIES

"These walnut sandies are the best!! I love making these for Christmas because I can color half of the dough green and half of it red. If you want melt in your mouth cookies, these are it!"

INGREDIENTS / DIRECTIONS

Set 1
1 c. butter
½ c. powdered sugar, sifted
2 T. honey
½ t. vanilla

Set 2
2 c. all purpose flour
¼ t. salt
¾ c. chopped walnuts

Set 3
2 c. powdered sugar

Tools: medium bowl,   large bowl,   electric beater,   non-stick cookie sheet or paper

Preheat oven to 325 degrees.

1. Mix flour and salt in medium bowl.
2. Cream butter, sugar, honey and vanilla in large bowl.
3. Combine #1 and #2 to make a soft dough. Add walnuts.
4. Form balls slightly less than 1 inch. Space balls about 1 ½ inches apart onto non-stick cookie sheet (disposable non-stick cookie sheets are great).
5. Bake for 14-16 minutes till very lightly browned. As cookies are removed from baking sheet, roll them into the powdered sugar for coating. Let cool completely on a wire rack. Roll cookies again in the powdered sugar for a second coating. Makes about 4 dozen.
6. At this point, cookies may be frozen in freezer bags.

SUGAR COOKIES

"Here is a great sugar cookie recipe, courtesy of my friend Nancy. You simply roll the dough out onto the cookie sheet, decorate and bake. It is quite delicious."

INGREDIENTS / DIRECTIONS

Set 1	Set 2	Set 3
2 c. all purpose flour	6 ½ T. butter	1 T. milk
1 ½ t. baking powder	1/3 c. Crisco	1 ½ t. vanilla
¼ t. salt	¾ c. sugar	1 egg

Tools: medium bowl, large bowl, electric beater, plastic wrap, non-stick cookie sheet (without a lip)

1. In a medium bowl, stir together flour, baking powder and salt.
2. In a large bowl, beat butter and shortening for 1 minute. Add sugar and beat till light and fluffy. Add milk, vanilla and egg. Beat together till well combined.
3. Pour dry #1 into #2 and combine to make a soft dough.
4. Wrap dough with plastic wrap and chill in fridge at least 3 hours.

Preheat oven to 375 degrees.

5. Working with a small batch of dough, roll onto ungreased cookie sheet 1/8 to ¼ inch thick. Cut out shapes with cookie cutter.
6. Remove excess dough and save for the next batch
7. Decorate with colored sprinkles.
8. Bake till nicely browned, 8-10 minutes.

SWEET POTATO CASSEROLE

"The best kinds of dishes, to me anyways, are the ones you can enjoy as a dessert on its own, or as part of the entrée. Well, this casserole really does it!! It is also one of Nancy's recipes and it's absolutely delicious with potatoes, turkey and gravy."

INGREDIENTS / DIRECTIONS

FILLING

<u>Set 1</u>
3 c. mashed, sweet potatoes
2 eggs
¼ c. milk or ½ c. heavy cream
¾ c. sugar
¼ t. cinnamon
1 ¼ t. vanilla
½ stick unsalted butter, melted

Tools: *non-stick spray, medium bowl, electric beater, 9-10 in. pie plate*

Preheat oven to 350 degrees.

1. Spray pie plate with non-stick spray.
2. Combine all ingredients in a medium bowl and beat with electric beater till well mixed.
3. Pour into pie plate.

TOPPING

<u>Set 1</u>
½ c. sugar
¼ c. flour
½ c. unsalted butter, softened
1 – 1 ½ c. halved pecans

Tools: *medium bowl*

1. Combine sugar, flour and butter with fingers.
2. Add pecans and blend well.
3. Press topping onto filling and bake for 45 minutes.
4. After 45 min., if a crisper, more browned topping is preferred, broil for a few minutes. WATCH THIS CAREFULLY. It only takes a short time and may burn if not attended to.

GUAM

Where America's day begins!
Tano' I man Chamoru

Dankolo na si Yu'us Ma'ase

To my fellow Chamorros,

I am so proud to call myself Chamorro. I am so proud to have been born and raised on Guam. It is my hope that we continue to preserve, promote and share our traditions and our heritage in all aspects of life.

Thank you to all who have done your part in sharing our food. Thank you for the food you provide at fiestas, weddings, christenings, nobenas, funerals, birthdays and bbqs. Thank you to those who organize and contribute to the Guam Liberation celebrations held annually throughout the world. Thank you to those Chamorros living off island who open their hearts and their homes to our soldiers. Thank you to those Chamorros on Guam and abroad who open their hearts and their homes to visitors such that they move on and remember how delicious our food is and remember our giving hospitality. God Bless the Chamorro people throughout the world, their families and their friends.

Biba Chamorro

Biba Guam

Places to eat on Guam

Chotde, Anigua   671-477-1524

The place to buy your favorites: empanada, doughnuts, pastit, buchi buchi, sandwiches, bread, titiyas etc! It is a beautiful drive from Yigo to Anigua, 6 a.m. in the morning, no traffic, and fresh goodies awaiting!

Onedera's Store, Dededo   671-632-7369

My parents love this stop for breakfast.

Hot dog stand, East Agana

The best hotdogs you'll ever have! Located by the beach, just off the road on East Agana.

Hot dog stand II, Malojloj

In Malojloj, great German bratwursts and they have got burgers too! Take a trip around the island, you'll see it.

KFC, Guam

Think it's odd to list this restaurant? If you have been on Guam, you should know why! You will not get red rice and fina'denne' at any other KFC that's for sure (if you find one, let me know). Sometimes, you just want red rice and fina'denne fast!!

Mc Donald's, Guam

Try asking for spam and rice anywhere else!! They'd think you are crazy!

Jamaican Grill, Chamorro Village   671-472-2000

Has been my favorite since the first location opened at Chamorro Village. Red rice, fina'denne', bbq ribs or chicken or fish, and their salsa......yum. Of course, they do have other items on their menu, but I always order the same thing, it is that good!

Shirleys, Tamuning   671-646-2288

A great place for breakfast: fried rice, spam, Portuguese sausage etc.

Esmeralda, Alupang Beach Tower   671-649-9666

A buffet that serves fried rice and other breakfast items! I hear they also have great tempura for lunch.

VIP, Asahi Building in Tumon   671-649-3222

If you want some delicious, fried, honey walnut shrimp, this is the place to go. Warning: order the large size, in fact, order two.

Chamorro Village

Shop, be entertained, eat, go to Chamorro Village.

Micronesia Mall

For those who have not been to the mall lately, it has expanded, including the food court. Good place to go for some quick red rice, fina'denne' and choice of meat.

GPO

Though we all have fond memories of when it was Gibsons, another great place to go to eat, similar to the mall's fare.

Chamorro Party, Any Village, Guam

Save the best for last, nothing like it, the place to eat on Guam!!

Fiestas

If you want to experience Guam food at its best, attend a Chamorro wedding or baptismal. If you happen to be on Guam, Saipan, Rota, California, Washington, Texas, the Carolinas or any other place with lots of Chamorros, go to the fiesta!! You'll find the ultimate in Chamorro feasts. A village fiesta is a celebration of the patron saint of the village, celebrated during the weekend:

JANUARY

> Tumon, 2nd weekend
>> Blessed Diego Louis San Vitores

> Chalan Pago, 3rd
>> Nuestra Senor de la Paz y Buen Viaje

> MongMong, 4th
>> Nuestra Senor de las Aguas

FEBRUARY

> Maina, 1st
>> Lady of Purification

> Yigo, 2nd
>> Our Lady of Lourdes

MARCH

> Inarajan, 3rd
>> Chamorro month: look out for events bound to showcase Chamorrow food.

APRIL

Barrigada, 1st
San Vicente

Agafa Gumas, 4th
Santa Bernadita

Merizo, 1st Sunday after Easter
San Dimas

MAY

Inarajan, 1st
St. Joseph the Worker

Malojloj, 2nd
San Isidro

JUNE

Tamuning, 2nd
St. Anthony

Toto, 4th
Immaculate Heart of Mary

JULY

Agat, 3rd
Our Lady of Mt. Carmel

Agat, 5th
    Santa Ana

Guam Liberation
    Celebrations held throughout the world celebrating Guam's liberation from the Japanese during WWII. Look for this event in your area!! It's a great place to have fun, bump into old friends, and make new ones.

AUGUST

Tamuning, 1st
    St. Victor

Piti, 2nd
    Assumption of Our Lady

Barrigada, 3rd
    San Roke

Agat, 4th
    Santa Rosa

SEPTEMBER

Canada Barrigada, 1st
    San Ramon

Agana, 2nd
    Dulce de Numbre de Maria

Talofofo, 3rd
    San Miguel

Mangilao, 5th
    Santa Teresita

OCTOBER

Yona, 1st
    St. Fancis Assise

Umatac, 2nd
    San Dioniseo

Sinajana, 4th
    St. Jude

NOVEMBER

None, but there will still be Chamorro bbq with the turkey!

DECEMBER

Agana Heights, 1st
    Our Lady of the Blessed Sacrament

Dededo, 2nd
    Santa Barbara

Agana, 2nd
    Our Lady of Camarin

Santa Rita, 3rd
    Our Lady of Guadalupe

Agana, 4th
    Nino Perdido y Sagrada Familia

Guam History

Pre Spanish contact –
- - original inhabitants are suspected to have migrated from Indonesia & Malaysia
- - excellent craftsmen, fishers and hunters
- - superb seamen
- - very strong matrilineal society
- - latte stones are found only on Guam and the Marianas Islands

1521   Ferdinand Magellan discovers Guam

1565   General Miguel Lopez de Legazpi claims Guam for Spain

1668 – 1815
        Guam is an important stop for the Spanish trade route

1898   U.S. gains control after the Spanish American War

1941   December 8
         Japan attacks Guam, WWII, Japanese occupation

1944   July 21
        Guam liberation by the U.S.

1950   Organic Act of Guam – unincorporated organized territory of the U.S.

Present – still a United States Territory; a major station for the United States Armed Forces

Index

Afterward

I have had a blast writing this book. I am so excited to put a book out there with Chamorro recipes that actually work. There was many a time where I would try a local recipe and end up with a flop. I am thrilled to share my recipes, in particular my recipes for guyuria, latiya and roskette. These are my pride and joy of all recipes included here.

It is my hope that you enjoy this cookbook. For more information regarding the contents of this book or if you would like to contact me, please email me at pquinene@paulaq.com.

21678861R00073

Made in the USA
Middletown, DE
08 July 2015